OPP!

Other People's Problems

Robert L. Harris

HATCHBACK Publishing
GENESEE, MICHIGAN

OPP! Other People's Problems
©2017 Robert L. Harris

All Rights Reserved. No parts of this publication may be reproduced or transmitted in any form or by any means, electronic or mechanical, or any information storage or retrieval system, without prior permission of the publisher or author.

Published by
HATCHBACK Publishing
Genesee, Michigan 48437
Since 2005

The views, opinions and words expressed in this book are those of the author and do not necessarily reflect the position of HATCHBACK Publishing LLC or its owners

ISBN 978-0-9988295-5-5

Printed in USA
10 9 8 7 6 5 4 3 2 1

For Worldwide Distribution

Dedication

Much like everything in life, I thank God. Just believing in Him makes all things possible.

This book is dedicated to my Mom and Dad, Robert and Ozzie Harris who are now in Paradise

To my Daughter, Tracy and Husband, Curtis

To my Grandchildren:
London, Dakota, Denver and Sicily

Contents

Introduction...5

1. Other People's Problems.....9
2. Most of Us Were Taught.....13
3. Poverty...A Way of Life.....17
4. Rich and Powerful.....21
5. Do What's Necessary.....25
6. Tower of Strength.....29
7. Indicating We Have Money.....33
8. Lose a Friend.....37
9. Innocent OPP.....41
10. Marriage and Relationships.....43
11. Starting a New Relationship.....47
12. Our Children.....51
13. We Live in a Complex World.....55
14. Getting Rid of OPP.....59
15. Conclusion.....65

Author Bio...69

Introduction

I wrote this book out of a desire to help someone understand if OPP is an issue in your life, there may be some answers to possibly help. It is not my intention to criticize or ridicule what someone may do. I believe each person does what that feel is suitable for that situation.

Not all OPP is bad. It is only when it reaches a certain point that may turn into a problem for you. I've studied and paid attention to OPP most of my life, much like a scientist who might study the behavior of ants.

This matter occurs in the lives of most. I have done my share. I know most of the time it has caused me problems but like anything else, you live and learn. I'm not complaining, I'm only explaining. It took me a while to understand and perfect a way to better deal with matters that involved me and someone else.

There is a formula which if worked in these guidelines, what you do for someone else may not seem such a sacrifice.

Like anything, it may take a while to learn. When doing for others it is best if you are ready, willing and able. If any of the three are missing, maybe you should not do anything. This structure works best.

This book is for anyone who may consider OPP to be an issue in their life. Learn and enjoy!

OPP!

Other People's Problems

1

OPP
Other People's Problems

There is something most of us may have in our lives, OPP or other people's problems. Much like a thief in the night, it may lurk just around the corner. Rich, poor, white, black, prominent or ordinary, it does not matter - each of us at one time or another had or are having this issue. Some may spend a lifetime coping with other people's problems, while others may not have this problem at hand, only to have it one day thrust upon you. It is something that may disrupt your life but some may not realize this fact. Until you realize it, it may one day cost you considerably.

You see, we believe we should help our fellowman and this may be true. In fact, if we all did, this world would be a better place. This may go deeper if it involves relatives. I'm sure most of us don't mind helping someone in need if we could afford to do so. And we all want to be appreciated for what we do when we help someone. The problem may be the things we do for others may get out of control and become unmanageable causing us, who do all we can, to have problems ourselves. I call this compounded - theirs plus yours equals yours minus theirs.

Each of us at some point may need help and may rely on others for support. We rely on family and friends for advice, opinions, decision-making, comfort, and financial aid. It is how many things get done. If we should help in these matters and things go well, we have a good feeling knowing we made a difference. All too often we lend ourselves to others and things don't go the way it should. When this happens we may feel angry and hurt. We have this let-down feeling and we may not want to help again. It's like cosigning and getting stuck with the bill.

A friend you have known for a long time is having troubles and he is behind in his mortgage. Unless someone helps, he may lose his home. He is your best friend so you have decided to help. You have now taken on other people's problems. Unless it all goes well, this may be a good deed gone bad you are now held accountable for. It is a possibility you may lose your friendship or be greatly inconvenienced since his problems are not your own because it did not turn out well. You now have his problem. Who wants that?

One thing you should never do is lend if you can't afford to suffer the loss should something go wrong. If you do it, you may find yourself out on a limb, probably a small limb at that.

I believe it is important you trust someone when doing favors, trusting not just their word but also their judgement. One may have good intentions but have poor judgement. Because of this, you may suffer. I, by no means, am recommending not doing for others. What you do is entirely up to you. However, I recommend having a certain kind of policy. That is, do right by me, you may come again. Do wrong, you no longer have me as your source of help. You are no longer in my favor circle. To not do this, you are allowing the foolishness to continue. Please cultivate your circle and help stamp out misunderstandings.

As a child, I learned the effect of other people's problems. I was raised the oldest of ten children and because of the size of our family alone, there were hard times. I sometimes went hungry. My mother was a good woman and deeply religious. She believed in helping others and did so tremendously. Her motto was, "Blessed is the cheerful giver". When people needed something they often turned to my mom. My dad, also a good man, was the sole supporter. He did all he could to make ends meet. Because of my mom's beliefs, the struggles were intensified.

My mom had a friend in particular who she helped for years. My mom and dad often argued because of this woman. One day she acquired a large sum of money. One would think she would have thanked my mom and given her something for the years of help. She did just the opposite. Under the cover of darkness, she upped and moved never to be heard from again. Sad to say, this may be typical behavior of other people's problems gone wrong. Some, not all, may do just the same.

2

Most of Us Were Taught

It was at a young age when most of us were taught responsibility. We were taught to look out for self and take care of our own affairs. Some perfected this while others didn't. These are mainly the people who need help.

Because you were the one who learned to be responsible, you did what was necessary to achieve all you have. You may have a good job, nice home, cars, recreational toys and maybe even a little money. Why? Because of your actions, you earned it. What may lurk in your comfortable world is other people's problems. Someone has a problem and they want you to solve it. Most of the time it is that irresponsible person we all seem to have in our lives. I've seen it many times. What you have may now be in jeopardy. The help someone needs may come at an inconvenient time or when you least expect it. It may be hard on you to help. Hopefully it is not that bad.

Things we do to help whether little or tremendous is at some sacrifice we make. If a loved one has a problem and you need to help, how far are you willing to go? Can you afford to do anything without a great incontinence to yourself? Is what you do really going to help? It does you no good to do things that may harm you in the long run.

To rise above some of this you can't have indecisions about what you do or may not do. You must do what is best for all involved. And if something is being asked of you and your answer is no, you may have made the best decision.

We live day by day surrounded by family and friends. Some may have problems. Let's be honest, a great deal of this is our kids. The fact that they are kids, they may be a little irresponsible. This can cause many problems for parents. Some may make terrible choices, I know I did. At such a young age they may not fully understand the effects of bad choices. They sometimes feel they are grown and they are not likely to listen. So you, as a parent, are on standby for what mistakes they make.

A young person out on their own may have a minimum wage job and buy an expensive car.

Their logic is they need something to get around in. This is true. We all need transportation. What may not resonate with this young person is their overall expense having such a car. If it is a fairly nice car, payments can be tremendous. Not to mention insurance. Because of their youth, many don't obey traffic laws. They get one or two tickets and their insurance goes through the roof. The contract they have for the car probably has a long future. They may not have considered other expense. If they are in school, that is an expense all its own. Do they have money for any maintenance the car may need? Although they have a job, it may not be all that secure. Many things can go wrong. If that happens, eventual they are in over their heads. Now they need help and may turn to you, their parents. Suddenly their problems become yours.

The right thing for that kid to have done pertaining to a car was to have paid cash if at all possible. The car may not be new, however, not having a large monthly payment would give him the money to now fix anything that may be wrong with the car. A new car that has been financed has to have full coverage. A vehicle that is your own, you have a choice to which coverage you choose. This alone may lessen burdens all around.

I would be willing to bet if this kid needed his parent's help, he may be more likely to get it. This is simply because the parents may realize they have raised a sensible child. Whatever money there may be, there is something good to be said for a young person who thinks this way.

I hope no one is under the assumption kids should do the smart thing, they won't. As parents we should do our best teaching our kids to be practical. If you don't take the time and effort of helping them learn, you may someday regret what you have failed to teach.

3

Poverty...A Way of Life

Poverty is a way of life for many. Some people barely get by. They face day by day struggles. Some merely exist. Poverty and despair is the world they live in.

This fact may be the reason they need help. Some are good people who just may be caught in a period of hard times. It maybe they simply don't have food. Because they are good people, if you are able to do something for them then do so. Any help you give them may make a difference.

The flip side to this is, not everyone who needs help is a worthy candidate. We live in a world filled with confusion and chaos. Many people are caught up in this. Some by choice. They choose to live the fast life. Some embrace it. As a result of their way of living, these people often need help as well.

The world is filled with drugs, alcohol, gambling, and gangs. There are many things that may corrupt someone. Some may not realize the reality or consequences they may face as a result of what they do. When things go wrong for them and they are in over their heads, they may turn to you for help. Should you help? You must decide. I will say it may not be in your best interest to help. That person has chosen that way of life and they may have continuous troubles. If you choose to help, it may not do much good because the problem may repeat itself. If that person has adapted to that way of life, it is their choice, not yours, so I believe you shouldn't get involved. Once you have helped, you may have set yourself up for them to come again. The more you do for them may make it harder to refuse if or when you decide not to help them anymore.

Try and see it this way, do for those who need it, other than the above, if you want to have less chaos and confusion they bring to you. If anything, teach irresponsible people you won't be a part of their bad choices. They must be held responsible for their own actions. By all means, if possible, this will keep their problems, which can easily become yours, at bay.

You have to realize the life they have chosen can costs you dearly. Some of these problems, I realize stems from poverty. Be a soldier in the war on poverty which always doesn't consist of having money. It may consist of your effort to stamp out foolish thinking. Do your best and help someone realize they may rise above the poverty if they so choose. Help them to understand there is a right and wrong way to accomplish what they want. You don't want what you neglected to teach to come back on you. So maybe what you try to teach someone is for your own sake as well as theirs.

The consequences of what someone does these days can be horrific. In some cases, what someone has done may come back on you and rock your world. You must fight for the privilege to not be misunderstood. Do what you can to help others understand this. You may help save their life and the life you save may be your own also.

4

Rich and Powerful

Rich and powerful people may be affected by other people's problems as well as average people. Because of their wealth, they may solve problems differently. Should something occur that involves a loved one or friend, they simply pay to have the matter go away which makes it easier for them. Because the average person doesn't have the same means, we may have to take care of the issue head on.

However, there can be some things money won't solve. If you decide to get involved, in your attempt to help, be careful. You may not be able to save them. What needs to be realized is some things people may do may cause a tall building to topple on you. Other people's problems does not discriminate. It is equal opportunity. Many things have a trickle- down effect which can hurt the person trying to help. Although you care about a person, there may be nothing you can do for them. They may just have to face the full responsibility for what they have done.

I once watched a western that I will never forget. There was this rich and powerful cattle baron who owned the town and the people in it. Everyone worked for him. He also owned the law. He had one son. Although somewhat ruthless and spoiled, his dad loved him. The dad raised him to be tough. The son did not quite measure up to the dad's expectation, nevertheless he loved him and would do anything for him.

One day while in another town, the son committed a terrible crime. Afterward he went back to the town his father owned. With a feeling he was above the law, he didn't think his crime would follow him. Even if it did, he felt his father would take care of it as he had done many times before. The sheriff of the town tracked the son to the town the father owned with a warrant for his arrest. When he got there he was greeted with elements that objected to the arrest, the town people and mainly the dad. The dad, who was used to having his way, was not about to have anyone take his son.

The dad, realizing his son was guilty, was trying to reason with the sheriff. He pleaded with the sheriff to not take his only son. This did nothing to change the fact his son committed the crime and he was going to answer for it. First the dad tried to buy the sheriff off. When that didn't work, he followed it with threats and an ultimatum for the sheriff to leave town or else he may be killed.

The dad was determined the only way someone was going to take his son was over his dead body. And then was the showdown and the sheriff, a faster drawer, killed the dad. The dad probably never thought this could happen.

The dad who was rich and powerful was brought down by his son's doings. Sometimes, in some situations, we may be unable to save them. As he laid dying, I imagine his last thoughts may have been how could something like this happen.

5

Do What's Necessary

Most people do what's necessary to enhance the quality of their lives. We educate ourselves, get jobs, do smart things with money, get married and have families. We do these things in pursuit of happiness. We hold to responsibilities and try to do what's right. Life is what we make of it and with this in mind, we do all we can to ensure things go well. Sometimes, because of all of our efforts, things work out!

I've known people like this only to have someone bring issues they may have which disrupts everything that's going well for them. I know someone who has for years been bombarded with a relative's problem. They put off things they wanted to do for the sake of this other person. I have done so, maybe not to that extent, nevertheless, many have.

The help we give for others affects us. No matter how we may see it, it does. Depending on the point of view, it can have small or great effects. Again, I am not saying don't help anyone. Help if you need to. Just understand what you do in life matters. You bear the outcome. It's like other people's problems loom just above the horizon no matter who you are, your situations or what you may have. Whether today, tomorrow or in the future, you will be confronted…so brace yourself.

If you have anyone in your life, such as a son, daughter, brother or sister, and you feel that you have a obligation. Be wise about what you may do for them. It's unfair for you to do something for someone and it causes you great harm. Sacrifices can cause you to do what you do then you miss out. Or it may mean you can't do for anyone in a great extent. You may be able to help someone short term. It is the long term you need to be worried about. If you have a situation which may need your long term help, please consider just how much you are able to do. Try and set a strategy that may work for them as well as you.

Hopefully, whatever may come your way in the terms of other people's problems is manageable. Everything that happens is not terrible. You may be spared many scenarios of what you may have to do for someone. It is my hope, anyone that may have other people's problems in their lives can deal with it in a way that is good for their peace of mind. Isn't that what we all want?

6

Tower of Strength

Some people are towers of strength although they may not realize it. These are the people who seem to have all the answers. They may be someone who is knowledgeable, fairly educated, and have all types of resources. They manage their affairs in a way that is obvious to everyone. This person has a nice home, cars, and tools which everyone seems to borrow because they have none of their own. This person takes pride in his accomplishments. He enhances whatever goes on with him to stay on top of things.

All of these are reasons to feel good about oneself. I agree this is a great way to be and if everyone was like this, we would have less problems from one another. Unfortunately, not everyone is.

The problems a tower of strength may have is people realize your strength. Therefore, someone who may be less fortunate and need something, they turn to you. Because of this fact, you may be bombarded with other's issues. Even if it is only when someone has a problem, they call you to vent because they feel you have the answers. When someone calls you with their problems, you listen and your day may have been disrupted. It takes time to listen to someone's problems. What they want may be simple advice and that is fine. We all may do this. One may feel okay that someone may think highly enough of them to ask for advice.

If someone calls you with a problem and you advise them with information which may help, you may have helped solve something. You can now feel you have a sense of purpose. Your being a tower of strength has made a difference to someone.

What we do to help others may not be the problem. The problem may be what we do to help can become overwhelming. One may not realize people may thrive on your strength. Unless you realize this fact and arm yourself with ways to keep some of this at bay, you may be bombarded with people wanting you to do for them. Like anything else, be careful what you start. Be careful of how much you do for anyone who may depend on you because you may have it hard should you feel a need to cut them off.

Beware of the money you have saved and someone knows about, they may need a loan. That extra car you have, someone may want to borrow it. The spare bedroom you have, someone may want to move in. The extra parking space you are not using, someone may want to park there for God only knows how long. I am not trying to sound harsh or selfish. I am just speaking from experience which most of it turned out bad. It is great to be a tower of strength. I have been one most of my life. I had to get older to recognize when people see you this way, you may have to do tremendous things for them.

When you cosign for someone, that person is using your strength. When it goes well, your strength has been put to good use. I have learned even a tower may crumble. Over the years of doing for others, you get weak. You have made a career helping. You may have inadvertently done this for years. After you have helped resolve one issue after another, you may have made someone's life easier. The flip side of this is you may have set yourself on a path that in the end may destroy you. There is only so much help you can give. In the end, you have given all there is to give leaving little for you.

So take heed, if possible, don't betray this. You may have less other people's problems to deal with. Play dumb…act broke!

7

Indicating We Have Money

What we need to realize is most of the time when people need help, it will consist of money. Should you help, this may put you in a bind should something go wrong.

I once loaned money to a relative on Monday, their rent was passed due. It was not easy for me to do this but nevertheless I did. I explained to this person my rent was due on Friday. I thought they understood that once they paid me back, I would pay my rent. Friday came and went. This person was a no show. It left me in a bad way. It was that experience which changed my way of thinking. When lending on a promise, don't lend unless you can afford the loss. If you help others you need the same policy as the bank. If you pay back a loan you borrow from a bank, you may borrow again. If not, the bank will not care what the reason is. Should you need help again, you will be denied. Banks have money set aside for loans. Like a bank, if you can afford to do so, have an account for other people's problems. This may be the money set aside you use to help others.

When we help it is often at an inconvenience to us. If things go wrong you are now in a fix. Sometimes people will come to you for tedious as well as large favors. If you have another people's problems account, any favors you do should come from that account. This money set aside to help someone may save the hurt should something go wrong. You still help, only now you have different methods which may spare you the amount of aggravation. If you loan, do it from that account only. Never do anything that may offset this structured pattern. If you are paid back put the money back in this account. If you are not paid back, never loan to this person again. If possible, replace the money. Many things we do in life require strategies. Helping people should be no different.

If you receive a three thousand dollar tax return, it may be smart to set aside ten percent, three hundred dollars for other people's problems. You can believe someone knows about your tax return and they are going to need your help. People have a way of knowing you have something. You may be the blame. You may brag or boast.

I once bragged I had a few credit cards to a friend not realizing I was setting myself up to be asked for a favor. It did not take long before this person asked to borrow money to buy something. I thought I was off the hook when I told them I was broke until they responded I could use one of my credit cards. I've kept my mouth shut ever since. Unknowingly, you give visions of some prosperity and people can see what is apparent. So when they see jewelry, nice cars, beautiful homes, they evaluate by what they see. Because of this they now feel you may help them.

People are funny. When they see someone with a lot they may not realize this person may be in over their head in debt and may not have a dime to spare. Little attention is paid to someone who is not flashy. They do little that indicate wealth. They may not have the forty thousand dollar car, or the three hundred thousand dollar home. This person does not show expensive jewelry. Because there is little advertisement on their part, people may think they have nothing to offer and may not bother them. This may be the person who has it all.

I once had a friend who fell on hard times and had to move in with his dad. He got lucky and hit the lottery. He bought the best stereo on the market. His dad was a very inconspicuous type of person. He came home from work and once he saw the stereo, realizing how much it cost, wanted his son to get it out of the house. He did not want anyone thinking he had any money. The dad was very well off. He worked for the General Motors and had several rental properties. He was also a traveling musician. He could have afforded most anything he wanted. The dad may have learned along the way, the more people see what you have, the more they feel you can do for them. It doesn't pay to advertise and hopefully his son learned from this. I know I did.

None of this is to say you can't have things and enjoy life. After all, you have worked for it. It does suggest that you use discretion. Don't brag in any way to someone who may be in hard times. Don't go around people whose rent is past due with ten thousand dollars of jewelry on. Don't buy the most expensive things especially while others all around are having a difficult time.

8

Lose a Friend

I'm sure we have all heard friends and money don't mix. This may be true depending on the friend and their perception of the word. Everyone does not truly understand the meaning of being friends. Friends may be far and few. Sometimes they are hard to come by. All too often people may take for granted what you do for them. Some may feel because you are friends that it is your obligation to help if they need it. After all, that is what friends are for.

When doing favors, if things go well then there is no problem. You may feel good because you have helped. The problem is everyone does not do the right thing when someone does them a favor. This makes it bad all the way around. I don't believe these individuals realize just how nice it is to have an ace in the hole, someone to turn to if they should need help. Some may play on your kindness. Some may intentionally play you for what they can get out of you. Truth be told, you may lose a friend over favors.

We live in a world of misunderstandings. There is always someone who doesn't quite get it. They may very well ruin it for everyone. For some reason, there can sometimes be confusion that goes along with favors. You can very well lose a friend over something petty. Some of the things you may hear when something goes wrong is: "Oh, I forgot," or "I didn't remember that is what we agree to." Sometimes they won't answer the phone when you call them. Some may even get mad because they have to pay you back.

Think how nice it would be if everyone understood the "scratch my back - I'll scratch yours" concept. If everyone did, we would all have someone to turn to should we need help. We all know what we want in return when we do for others. We want their appreciation to say the least. We want whatever was agreed upon to go well. We want, if something should go wrong, that person to come to us in all sincerity and let us know what went wrong. The one who does the favor should never have to ask what the problem may be. It tears away at the friendship and may leave you not wanting to help again. It seems a no brainer, be considerate of what's been done to help you.

When I was a teenager, I had a friend I had known since kindergarten. He and I were real buddies, practically inseparable. We did many things together. One day it was my turn to pay for something. Because I had to go to the restroom I gave him the money to pay for me. He did and later I asked did I have any change. He said I didn't but I knew beyond a shadow of doubt I did. I remember the feeling I had knowing he cheated me. It was no more than a dime or two, nevertheless it was my change. I never said anything to him. Although we remained friends for years, I never completely trusted him again. Because of something so small, we never again had a total friendship. I didn't want what was so petty to destroy our relationship. This is typical to a fallout over something so small. Honesty and trust is the true meaning of a good relationship. Anything short of this is not a total friend.

9

Innocent OPP

When someone you are responsible or care for such as a child or maybe even an adult does something with no bad intention - it may have been an accident, carelessness or something they did not mean to do - this is innocent other people's problems. Although what they did may be unintentional, you may have to pay for it. It can be something like a child who breaks the neighbor's window, it very well may have been an accident - nevertheless, you as the parent may be held responsible.

Whether we realize it or not, we live in jeopardy of what someone we are responsible for may do. Most kids really have no idea the magnitude of a problem they may bring to their parents. Most of the time, parents are caught off guard and may be totally unprepared for the things that may happen. If one can afford to, it may not be a bad idea to set some money aside for the unexpected. Not many can do this, however if you could it may help save you in the long run. If nothing happens by the time a child reaches eighteen, it may be a good idea to give them part of the money you saved. It could be sort of a reward for what they did not do.

I know someone who had a fifteen year old son who was a good kid. He went to school every day, got good grades, did not hang with the wrong crowds, and wanted to attend college. He was a good child in most ways. One day he took his parents' car keys without permission. He may have intended to just go around the block or maybe to McDonalds. Unfortunately he got into an accident. With being underage, no driver's license and no insurance, his parents were suddenly faced with the nightmare of their son's doings. The parents worked hard for what they had and now they had to bear the responsibility of what their child had done. It must have been devastating.

It does no harm to try and protect yourself from things a child may do. Have an open mind. They are children and anything may happen. It's all a part of life. Try and be prepared when Old Man Trouble calls.

10

Marriage and Relationship

Because of other people's problems, many marriages and relationships have been disrupted as well as destroyed. Couples may have matters between them they are dealing with. They may have gotten together and are trying to sort out what works for them. They may be financially just getting by. Whatever the case may be, I'm sure they may want to contain whatever they have between themselves. Add other people's problems to this and it may intensify their efforts to be together. They may be young, just starting out, and may not realize the problems this may cause them. This does not only apply to new couples. People who have been together for years may have other people's problems in their lives. It has caused serious problems for many.

I have gone through this and some of it was quite bad. I was once married and my wife and I were doing okay. We were getting by but not much more. My wife had a friend who did not have a washer or dryer. Because we did, this friend and her husband would use ours on a regular basis. They would use it while I was away because they knew I would not go for it. They played on my wife's gullibility. To top all of that, they both had jobs. Why buy your own when you can use someone else's? Once I realized this it infuriated me. I had to put a stop to it.

It is sad to think some people may do this which makes it bad for others. Things like this causes couples to be at odds with one another. Some of it can even be the straw that breaks the camel's back. My advice to anyone in a relationship, if you want to keep it, beware, as sure as the sun rises, other people's problems may be coming into your world. You can find yourself in arguments and disruptions. It can also cause disagreements in things you may have planned. Separations and divorces can all be brought on by others. Some people may not even realize the trouble they have caused you. Some are just inconsiderate and some don't care. Anyone who has gone through this knows what I mean. Anyone who hasn't may soon find out.

For your sake, and for the sake of your relationship, hopefully you and your mate see eye to eye as to what you will do when something like this occurs. Whether it be neighbor, friend, siblings, parents or in-laws, decide what means more to you. It is you who will have to bear the consequences if you have chosen wrong. You will have allowed someone to destroy what you had.

11

Starting a New Relationship

We may all have good intentions and feel we help. May be we do. Only you can determine that. You also may feel you didn't do much good. If this is your feeling, no need to be bitter. Hopefully your lessons have been learned.

Sometimes other people's problems may take time before you realize the effect it has had on you. Hopefully you have learned to be careful about what you get involved in. Many times people ignore warning signs they should have paid attention to only to have regrets later. The fact is you may have good intentions and other people may not. They simply may not understand what's right. It is up to the individual to know what's best. If you believe whatever you do will not turn out right, maybe you shouldn't do it. Be the wiser and leave it alone.

In many new relationships, some people don't consider what problems the other may have and what they may bring into the relationship. When they get together, maybe they have fallen in love. When someone is in love, they may only have one side of the story - they want to be with that person. They feel they have met their soulmate. Or someone may just be lonely and want someone to be with. In this case, the problems of the other person may be overlooked or ignored. When you get with someone, their problems become yours. It can destroy whatever chance at happiness you may have. It is only you who decides who you want to be with and then live with that decision.

I knew a guy who met someone and fell in love. He was blinded by it. He wanted to get married and did so. He really didn't take the time to consider the things he should have. All he wanted was this woman. It so happens this woman was deeply in debt. The car she drove had serious mechanical problems. If that's not bad enough, the car was on the verge of repossession. She had terrible credit and was a shopaholic. It did not take long before her problems overwhelmed them both completely. Eventually, of course, this destroyed the marriage.

As much as we may want someone in our lives, give yourself a fighting chance if you want to be happy. One day you may have to make that choice and hopefully you do what's smart. All too often, people get with someone that are no good for them. No one certainly can stand in judgement of this because we may not know the whole story. However, they may find in the long run it doesn't work well. The overall faults of someone's lacking may eventually destroy it all.

Think if you should decide to be with someone. Hopefully you are equally matched. And so beware, he who picks a rose must accept the thorn that grows.

12

Our Children

Our children may be one of the greater causes of other people's problems in our lives. Whether they are younger or older they cause problems that parents have to deal with. I know, once they are grown they are on their own. Many parents, including myself have said this. It has been my experience throughout the years and I've seen on occasion, too often our kids make poor choices. I don't believe they mean to do it but as a result, you may be on military standby for whatever may go wrong.

I know I was on standby all throughout my daughter's puberty years. Suddenly, overnight she turned wild and crazy. I mean she was one hundred and fifty miles away at house parties, and hanging with strange folks. I hardly recognized her. She was on the go and I couldn't tell her anything. For me, it was unbelievable and I spent many nights worried. Fortunately, for the both of us, nothing too bad happened.

The truth is some young people make bad decisions. It can be worse if they hang with the wrong crowd and are easily influenced or mislead. Good or bad things can happen. It may simply depend on who they are hanging with. Sometimes a good kid who is with the wrong people, because of what they see and hear, may get into trouble. You may have taught that child well for them to fall victim to bad influence.

There are many scenarios that may cause problems for parents. I often wonder parents who are spared realize how good they have it. Imagine that, a child never coming to you for anything because they are completely on their own. It has got to feel great.

On the other hand, you may be at the mercy of your child's decisions. You have a daughter you have raised well. She has been nothing but a source of pride and inspiration all her life. You love her dearly. One day she meets and falls for "Mr. Wrong". You, as her dad, know this guy is no good for her. Everything about him, in your opinion, spells bad news. You don't want your daughter him. You tell her your concerns and the reasons you feel the way you do. You tell her she would be better off to dump this guy. She doesn't understand it and she's in love. There is nothing you or anyone else can tell her. She wants to be with him no matter what. As her father you can only wish her well even though you know it simply will not work. A father can see things for his daughter, especially if she is in love and cannot see.

This is why a guy is a little afraid to meet a girl's dad. They do feel relieved if the dad approves of them. In some cases, if a dad does not approve a daughter's guy, if she is wise, she would consider that. Sometimes, father does know best.

So she takes off with the guy believing he is the one. Maybe years down the road she realizes she has made a bad choice. She wants out of the relationship but only now she has kids. There is no place she can really go except her parent's home. They certainly won't deny her. So the parents give her whatever help she may need.

If she has learned valuable lessons, you as a parent may not mind what you've done to help your daughter. If she does it again, her many problems may also become yours. Your leisure years may not be so leisure. Your life may be filled with crying babies that need Pampers and milk - just like you did for yours thirty years ago. That life time trip you planned to Hawaii, you may have to cancel. There may be no early retirement either. Your life could have a complete turn-around that may take years to sort out.

Everything our children do may not be this dramatic. We all make mistakes. That's a part of life. We must teach our kids common sense. Above all else we must teach them to be their own person and not be influenced by others.

I hope no one assumes kids should do what's right, they won't. It may take time to be able to distinguish what's right and what's wrong. Over time they may perfect their thinking. We can only hope what we have taught them serves them well. The better we have taught them the less chances they may come back for help.

At the time I didn't think so but eventually my daughter came back to her senses. Now I can take that trip.

13

We Live in a Complex World

Some of the things we do are not easy. Life puts demands on us. Still we do our best. There are all sorts of confusion which may make things seem a little mixed up. Take in account the high cost of living. Some mortgages and rent are twelve hundred dollars a month. Throw in the other things and this may be hard to maintain. If you are doing so, you probably don't have time to spare. Some people can't simply afford anything and they are barely getting by.

Good jobs may be hard to get and minimum wage does not pay for much. If there is a car payment, that alone can be your entire check. There is rent, food and whatever else you have to pay for. Gas prices have reached the stratosphere. Unless you have a high paying job or other means of having big money, you may just exist and nothing more. The quality of life is not good.

To rise above this, you must be somewhat exceptional. Not everyone is capable. It is because of this some people feel they have few choices. They must rely on others if they need help. Helping someone who really needs it is what we should do. You may need this one day. Some help we do is okay as long as it doesn't require too much.

The problem maybe sometimes we take on more than we should. You need to understand just how much you are able to do for someone should you have to and not go beyond that. If you are in a position where you can't do anything, then that's the spot you're in. You are in no position to take care of anyone if you can barely make it yourself.

If someone comes to you and you can't do for them, don't be afraid to say no. It may hurt you to do so. You may even be sorry that you can't help. That simply may be the way it is. Some people have no problem with the word no. Others, for whatever reason, find it hard to say it. To not say no when you should may not be the best thing for all involved.

Sometimes instead of one needy person you now have two. Everything should depend on your capability to help within your means and without tremendous sacrifice on your part. All too often some people feel like they are helping but you cannot save a drowning person. You can jump in to rescue them but you cannot unless you know what you are doing. If you don't know what you are doing you may drown as well.

What we do in efforts to help someone may be just as similar. People need to live within their means, whatever it may be. Not everyone can understand this. You see it all the time. Someone buys something they can't afford. They don't do things suitable for their situation. They may not make any attempt to better things for themselves. You may even try to recommend things they should do that might make things a little better for them. Your advice means little to them so they don't listen. These are the same people who find themselves in a bind and when they do, they need your help. Should you help? I don't know but I will say if you find yourself in this circle of people, you should find ways to protect yourself.

If this behavior is in your life for a long time, it will affect the quality of your life. You may be miserable because of it. For your own sake, do something. There is nothing wrong with someone who is looking out for themselves. Strong minded people are needed to keep things going. That's what makes the world go around. Save yourself for bigger, more meaningful and better things.

It is your choice to decided who, why, and if you should help.

14

Getting Rid of OPP

In daily life we face all sorts of problems. Whether it is big or small, you can't hardly go through a day problem free. Whether or not we realize it, problems are in every crack and crevices of our lives. Whether the plumbing has gone bad, the car won't start or something is wrong with the thermostat - these are just some of the things we face every day. For some reason life is set that way.

Most of us do what we can to handle whatever may come our way. These are responsible people that realize things occur and ready themselves to take issues head on. That being the case, I don't believe it's unfair to say they are somewhat deserving.

There is a quotation that says, *God helps those who help themselves.* I believe this to be true. You must do for yourself and not always rely on others.

Many things in your life may be going great. You have done what it takes to ensure this. All of your honest, hard work is paying off for you. You have done smart things. You have earned whatever you have, even if it is in abundance, you've worked for it. Because of this you have the means to enjoy life. Throw caution to the wind my friend, someone may take you out of that comfort zone.

Everything may be going really great for you. A sad reality is unless everyone who is in your circle, family or friend are doing okay, unless you are completely selfish, you may not be able to live that carefree life. It may be a little hard for you to enjoy that vacation in the Caribbean knowing someone you care about is about to be evicted. Or you have a loved one who is in trouble and may spend serious time in jail unless he gets a good lawyer. And who is to pay for this high profile attorney? If you are a compassionate and caring person who cares about others, although good, this may work against you.

In your endeavors for peace and tranquility, realize someone is out to take that away from you - whether it is intentional or not. It is up to you to protect yourself. Some people don't have this problem. These are the people who won't do a thing for anyone. I don't believe that is a nice way to be. These people better hope they never need help for themselves.

As much as you may want to help, you can't do it for everyone. Be selective. Help we do is either productive, meaning when you have done something for someone, there is some progress. They take what you did and use it in ways that matter which made things better and they are ready to move on. There is also a nonproductive help you do. The problem may repeat itself time and time again. What you did to help was futile and made things no better for anyone. This is the type of other people's problems you must eliminate. Also, you should steer clear of someone who may be ungrateful.

Have you ever started the day feeling great, in a good mood and there is nothing pressing you at the time? You decide to relax and watch some television. Just as you begin to absorb the relaxation, somebody stops by or the phone rings. This is the main carrier of bad news from which there is no escape. It is someone who has a problem. They need your help to solve it. So much for your carefree day.

We all seem to have that irresponsible person in our lives that's plain sorry and nothing ever goes right for them. They are never happy. The have one excuse after another. They really don't put much effort into things which may work for them. They are the carriers of bad news. Nothing ever seems to go in their favor. The Bad Luck Fairy has a hold on them. If they are in your circle and you get involved, suddenly what now bothers them bothers you.

You and you alone must decide what is to be eliminated when it comes to people. You had better put up a fight if some of this applies to you. Some you may have to put out of your favor circle because they may not have belonged there in the first place.

Over the years I have learned to perfect this way of thinking. Nevertheless, I sometimes still give in. I suppose I have inherited some of my mom's charitable ways. No one is suggesting to be cold or callous if someone needs your help. You may have to turn to someone yourself. The truth is we all need to learn to look out for one another. Until everyone understands this, one must work within the guidelines of what we should do. Don't let anyone dump on you. If you choose to help, do it in a way that is beneficial to each of you. You get gratitude, appreciation and a good feeling to know you have done meaningful help. And they get the help that may make a difference. It may be the help that saves them. This can work all around.

No one can free themselves from everything. However, you can do a process of elimination, sparing yourself from as much as possible and getting rid of stress others may put on you. Stress shortens life. It may be hard but you must not let too much of someone else's problems become your own.

15

Conclusion

It is not as important that someone understands your reluctance or refusal to help them as it is for you to understand your decision. Only you know what's best. It may be logical to loan someone five dollars and not logical to loan someone your car. It is our mission to teach. We need to help irresponsible people understand reality.

We must be able to distinguish nonsense from the ones who really need our help. Many people, especially the young, may not realize life is a series of problems. A great part of education is no more than being taught ways to deal with life and problems which we are sure to face. Anyone who does not understand may miss the entire point. If you fail to do so, you may take a wrong turn and just keep going. These are the ones we often have to help.

Many things rely on what you have been taught as a child. That's where it all starts. Some parents may misinterpret good parenting by spoiling their children. I am sure they are unaware but they try to make life so easy for them they may not help the child understand how difficult life can be. Many shelter their kids when they should teach them the harsh reality.

My dad scared the hell out of me. He told me he would pick me up in ten minutes and for me to be outside because he was in a hurry. I paid little attention to the ten minute part. I thought he was just talking. In ten minutes he was there. I wasn't and he left me. I had to walk home in the scary dark. This may sound a little harsh and probably shouldn't be done in today's crazy world. Nevertheless it worked. My dad took this opportunity to teach me something. That's the kind of man he was. He seemed to always have taught consequences if you did wrong. Today I can appreciate that. It taught me to be punctual. Many times I have made a point of being on time because of that experience. It made me realize either be there or be left behind.

Parents need to realize our kids run life's gauntlet and we can only hope the best for them. A gauntlet can go either way. You must teach kids the ability to hold their own. Don't always keep them in a fairy tale world and have them believe everything is simple because you so far have made it seem that way. Tough love is the better love.

You must prepare them to be independent and not rely on others so they don't become other people's problems. Your failure to do this may make you sad one day. In your efforts to be a good parent, you owe it to your kids to teach them things they will carry through life.

Some parents feel they are doing a good job because of their way of thinking. They don't want their child to want for anything. They don't want their child to go through anything they went through. I agree to spare them some of it. However, you should teach there's a difference in fact and fiction. For the parent not to understand that concept, they may be their child's worst enemy.

You as the parent must teach them the word no as well as yes sometimes. Put some type of stipulation on when your answer is yes like sometimes it comes easy and other times it does not. Like sometimes say no to what may be the smallest of things like can I have a quarter for the video game and then sometimes say yes to some big things like a pet tiger. What you are teaching them is being able to accept and learn to deal with the answer no and to be happy and appreciative for yes which they may feel they have earned. What you have taught them is the answer yes may not always come easy. They may have to work for it. This helps them not to have that let down feeling if someone refuses to do something for them. This may motivate their drive to be independent. This may also help them not to become other people's problems.

You have done a great job if it turns out this way. What they have learned may help throughout their life. You have done your part to raise your kids not to become other people's problems. What greater thing to leave your child once you are dead, other than the things you put in their heads.

If you look closely at people who seem to always be in the need of help, you may find they didn't learn certain things as a child. Their parents failed to teach them some valuable lessons.

I've known people like this and I've tried to talk to them. I've often found what I said to be true. In some cases, some of them were spoiled. I've heard people say when they were a kid they didn't want for anything. Once in the real world they were unprepared. They missed learning some of the important things. Mainly to be independent.

Author Bio

A Vietnam veteran, serving time in the Navy as a gunners mate, Robert Harris retired from General Motors after thirty years of service and now operates his own landscaping business.

Born in Chicago, Illinois, Robert now resides in Saginaw, Michigan. He is the proud father of a lovely daughter and four beautiful grandchildren.

To contact Robert for information or speaking engagements email:

rharris44.rhh@gmail.com

www.ingramcontent.com/pod-product-compliance
Lightning Source LLC
Chambersburg PA
CBHW060426050426
42449CB00009B/2163